ON VACATION

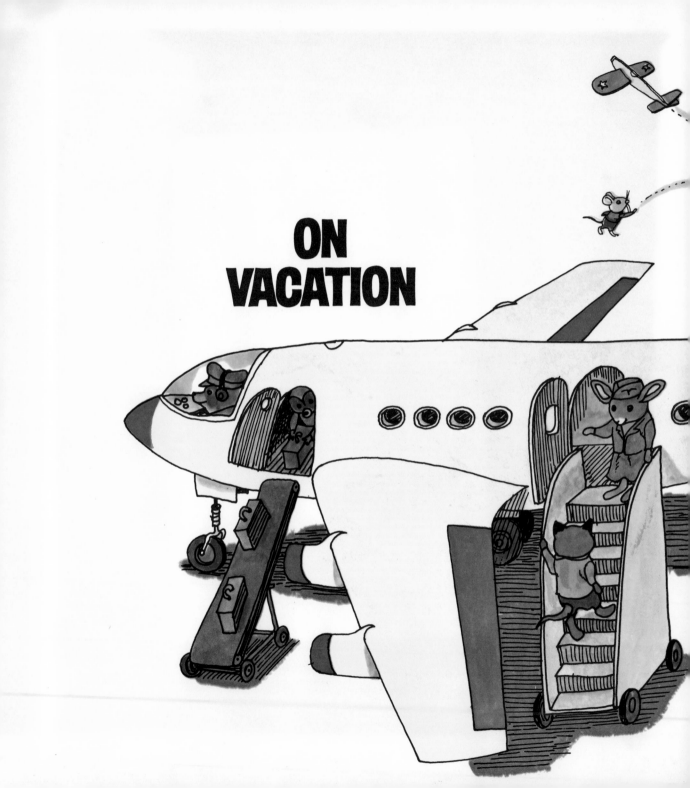

ON VACATION

with illustrations by
Richard Scarry

gb Golden Press • New York

Western Publishing Company, Inc.
Racine, Wisconsin

Library of Congress Catalog Card Number: 75-27089

ISBN 0-307-11823-1

Vacation Time

Vacation time is here. Everybody is going on vacation. Some go by train, some go by car, some take a ferryboat across the river.

Do you see Squeaky Mouse? He is going by raft.

Point to:

railroad track
railroad crossing
locomotive
car
raft
ferryboat

Happy Flying!

Cat is going far away for his vacation.
He is taking a jet plane. Cat goes in one door
and his suitcase goes in another door.

Look! Penny Pig has her own little airplane.
That's a nice way to travel!

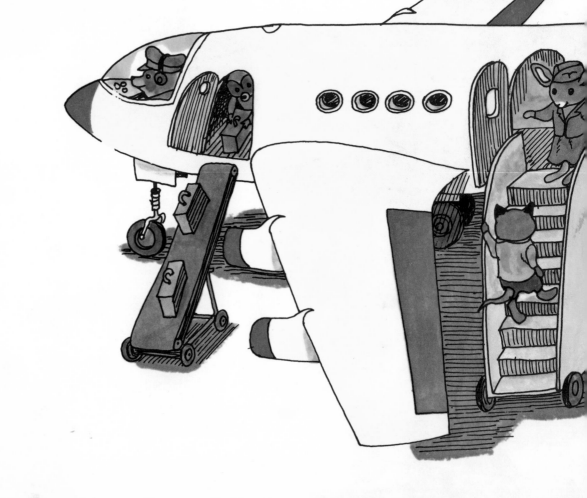

Do you see?

jet airplane
Penny Pig's airplane
pilot
tail
wing
wheel
propeller
wind sock
suitcases

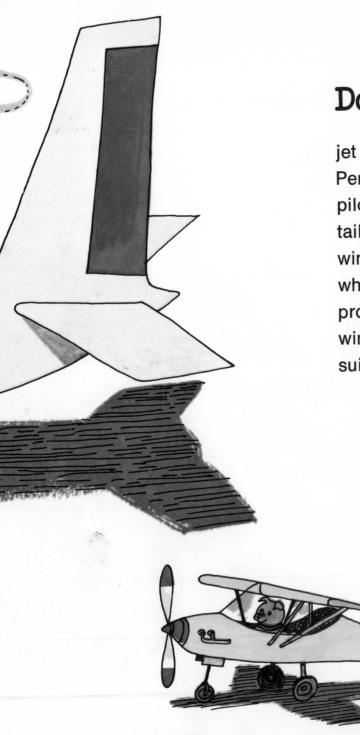

In the Mountains

Have you ever been to the mountains? You can play in the woods or wade in a mountain stream. You can sleep in a log cabin.

Do you see some mountain climbers on a cliff? Whoops! Look out! Something is falling. Can you see what it is?

Point to·

log cabin   knapsack
axe   mountain climbers
pine trees   cliff

At the Lake

Look at all the boats sailing on the lake!
The wind makes the sailboat go. A motor makes the
motorboat go. Do you see a rowboat? Do you know
what makes the rowboat go?

Look! There is Squeaky, sailing his raft!

Point to:

houseboat

speedboat

fishing boat

sailboat

motorboat

buoy

At the Beach

The Rabbits like to spend their vacation at the seashore. There are so many things to do at the beach.

Do you see?

beach chair	sand castle	sun
stairs	seagull	lifeguard
seashell	beach house	toy seahorse
umbrella	bathing suit	flags

Camping

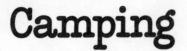

The Foxes are on a camping trip. They carried all of their things in the back of their car.

They have set up their tent, table, and cot. Mr. Fox is cooking supper on the grill. Later, they will go to sleep in their tent.

Do you see some guests coming for supper? Do you think the Foxes will be happy to see them?

Point to:

pickle	ants	grill
hot dogs	tent	picnic basket
car	cot	table

Special Days

Sometimes a special day comes
during a vacation.

Kitty's birthday comes during summer
vacation. Can you see Kitty's birthday cake?
How old is Kitty today?

Easter comes in the spring, when everything
is new. Then we see lots of chicks and
bunnies and Easter eggs. Can you see a
bunny painting an Easter egg?

Christmas comes during a vacation. We find presents for our family and decorate our tree. Christmas is not vacation-time for Santa Claus. He goes to work, bringing presents to children everywhere.

What can you see on the Christmas tree?

house   candy cane
bird   red ball
angel   striped ball
blue ball   lights

Winter Vacation

It is cold in the winter.
There is lots of ice and snow.

Can you see somebody skiing?

How many rabbits are riding on
a toboggan?

Who has a red sled?

Squeaky is throwing a snowball
at Bear. Bear is playing a game
called ice hockey. He slides over
the ice on his ice skates, pushing
the hockey puck with his stick.

Do you know what Raccoon is doing in that little
house? She has made a hole in the ice and is fishing
through it. I wonder if she will catch anything?

Point to:

skis
hockey puck
hockey stick
toboggan
ice skates
ski poles
sled
snowball
boots

Staying at Home

Bear is staying at home this vacation. But he is not lonely. Some of his friends are staying home, too. There are lots of things to do at home.

Bear's friends the kitten sisters are playing ring-around-the-rosy. They like the part where they all fall down best. Do you like that part, too?

Things to do at home

fly paper airplanes

play ring-around-the-rosy

have a tea party

play with a ball

help with the housework

go for a walk

More to do at home

Play a game with a friend.
Do you know the name of this game?
Bear has the black checkers and Rabbit
has the red ones. Bear is thinking
hard, but Rabbit is winning anyway.

Go to the playground with a friend.
Bear and Rabbit are playing on the seesaw.
First Bear goes up and Rabbit goes down.
Then Bear goes down and Rabbit goes up.
Then Rabbit stays up. He cannot get down.
Do you know why?

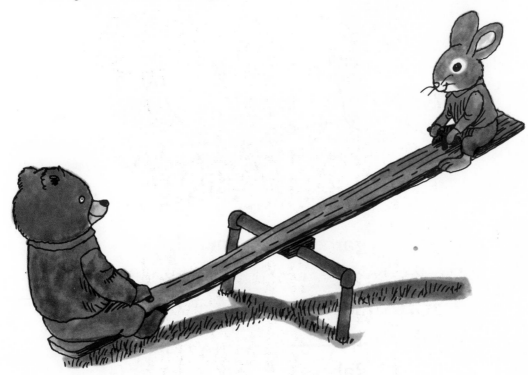

THE
END